BASICS OF A
BALANCED LIFE

Six BASICS OF A BALANCED LIFE

Carol Kent & Karen Lee-Thorp

NAVPRESS

BRINGING TRUTH TO LIFE

P.O. Box 35001, Colorado Springs, Colorado 80935

OUR GUARANTEE TO YOU

We believe so strongly in the message of our books that we are making this quality guarantee to you. If for any reason you are disappointed with the content of this book, return the title page to us with your name and address and we will refund to you the list price of the book. To help us serve you better, please briefly describe why you were disappointed. Mail your refund request to: NavPress, P.O. Box 35002, Colorado Springs, CO 80935.

The Navigators is an international Christian organization. Our mission is to reach, disciple, and equip people to know Christ and to make Him known through successive generations. We envision multitudes of diverse people in the United States and every other nation who have a passionate love for Christ, live a lifestyle of sharing Christ's love, and multiply spiritual laborers among those without Christ.

NavPress is the publishing ministry of The Navigators. NavPress publications help believers learn biblical truth and apply what they learn to their lives and ministries. Our mission is to stimulate spiritual formation among our readers.

FOR A FREE CATALOG OF
NAVPRESS BOOKS & BIBLE STUDIES,
CALL 1-800-366-7788 (USA)
OR 1-416-499-4615 (CANADA)

CONTENTS

INTRODUCTION

Heart Balance

I (Carol) laughed out loud as I read the article. The headline said, "Fast Pace Leads Us to Bad Health." A doctor had documented a new illness he called "The Hurry-Up Disease." He said we hurry to get up in the morning to hurry through the shower to hurry through breakfast to hurry to work in rush-hour traffic to hurry home during rush-hour traffic to hurry through dinner to hurry to watch the news to hurry to bed to hurry up and do the same thing over again the next day. (Try saying that sentence five times—fast!) I was out of breath by the end of reading his description of an average day. As he described the gerbil on the Wheel of Life, I realized the face on the gerbil was *mine!*

Wouldn't it be helpful if you could hire Jesus as your personal time-management consultant? He could look down your to-do list and say, "That item—that's a waste of time. This—now this is important. And *this* is okay, as long as it doesn't get in the way of *that.*"

Jesus and the Holy Spirit are eager to offer you their wisdom. And their fee is absolutely nothing (or absolutely everything, depending on how you look at it). That's what this study offers you: a chance to get Jesus' input on how to put your life in balance.

The first thing you need to know is that balance begins in your *heart,* the inner source of your thoughts, feelings, desires, and choices. In New Testament language, people think in their hearts, feel in their hearts, and choose with their hearts. Jesus says,

"No good tree bears bad fruit, nor does a bad tree bear good fruit. Each tree is recognized by its own fruit. People do not pick figs from thornbushes, or grapes from briers. The good man brings good things out of the good stored up in his *heart,* and the evil man brings evil things out of the evil stored up in his *heart.* For out of the over-flow of his *heart* his mouth speaks." (Luke 6:43-45, emphasis added)

Our words and actions flow from our hearts. If our outer lives (fruit) are unbalanced, then we need to look at the source of that fruit: the goals, desires, priorities, motives, passions, and beliefs in our hearts. Perhaps we have too many goals and they're in conflict with one another. Perhaps we have no goals and are letting ourselves be swept along from one activity to another. Maybe our hearts are cluttered with other people's goals for us.

In this study we'll look at the key question, "What's really important?" As we answer that question, we'll find out it's *not* important to "do it all"! If we first settle the question of what our heart attitude is toward God and other people, many of our balance issues will begin to make sense, and the decisions about what to cut out of our lives will become more clear.

This study is not meant to be one more item on your to-do list. You've already had enough stress today! This study is designed to help you relax and have fun as you make important decisions about the way you structure your life. So take a deep breath. Post yourself a note: I AM NOT A GERBIL. And settle in to hear what God is whispering to you.

How to Use This Guide

You were born to be a woman of influence. No—we don't mean a busybody or a queen bee, telling others what to do or making their lives revolve around yours. You were born to model your life on Jesus' life, and in so doing, be a model for others. Perhaps your influence will happen in a few quiet words over coffee, in a hug or a prayer. Don't say, "Not me—I'm barely treading water!" If you have the Spirit of God in your life, you have what it takes. God wants to influence people through you.

We've created these *Designed for Influence* Bible studies to draw out this loving, serving, celebrating side of you. You can use this study guide in your private time with God, but you'll gain even more from it if you meet with a small group of other women who share your desire to grow and give. The study is designed around the seven life-changing principles explored in Carol Kent's book, *Becoming a Woman of Influence.* These principles, which underlay Jesus' style of influencing others, are:

- Time alone with God
- Walking and talking
- Storytelling
- Asking questions
- Compassion
- Unconditional love
- Casting vision

Each of the six sessions in this guide contains these seven sections:

An Opening Story. When you see the word "I" in this guide, you're hearing from Carol. She begins each session with a story from her own life to let you know we're not making this stuff up in some spiritual hothouse; we care about these issues because we're living them. As you read these stories, look for a point of connection between your life and Carol's.

Connecting. Next comes your chance to tell your own story about the topic at hand. If you're studying on your own, take a few minutes to write down a piece of your life story in response to the questions in this section. If you're meeting with a group, tell your stories to each other. Nothing brings a group of women together like sharing stories. It's not necessary for each person to answer every question in the rest of the study, but each person should have a chance to respond to the "Connecting" questions. Sharing stories is great fun, but try to keep your answers brief so that you'll have time for the rest of the study!

Learning from the Master. The entire Bible is the Word of God. Yet Jesus Himself is the Word of God made flesh. The Bible studies in this series focus on Jesus' words and actions in the Gospels. You'll get to see how Jesus Himself grappled with situations much like those you face. He's the smartest guy in history, the closest to the Father, the one who understood life better than anyone else. This is your opportunity to follow Him around and watch how He did it. If you're meeting with a group, you don't need to answer the questions ahead of time, but it would be helpful to read through them and begin thinking about them. When your group gathers, ask for one or more volunteers to read the Scripture aloud. If the story is lengthy, you could take turns reading paragraphs. Or if you really want to have fun, assign the roles of Jesus and the other characters to different readers. Karen wrote the Bible study section of this guide, and if you have any questions or comments, you can e-mail her at bible.study@navpress.com.

A Reflection. This section contains some thoughts on the topic as well as some questions that invite you to apply what you've learned to your own life. If you're meeting with a group, it is helpful, but not necessary, to read the reflection ahead of time. When your group reaches this point in the study, you can allow people a few minutes to read over the reflection to refresh their memories. Talk about the ideas in this section that seem especially helpful to you.

Talking with God. This section closes your meeting if you're studying with a group. Inviting God to enable you to live what you've discussed may be the most important thing you do together. In addition to the prayer ideas suggested in this section, feel free to include your personal concerns.

Time Alone with God. This section and the next are your "homework" if you are meeting with a group. The first part of your "homework" is to take some time during the week to be with God. In this section you'll find ideas for prayer, journaling, thinking, or just *being* with God. If you're already accustomed to taking time away from the rush of life to reflect and pray, then you know how these quiet moments energize you for the rest of your week. If you've believed yourself to be "too busy" to take this time to nourish your hungry soul, then this is your chance to taste the feast God has prepared for you.

Walking with Others. The second part of your "homework" is to pass on God's love to someone else in some way. Here you'll sample what it means to be a woman of influence simply by giving away something you've received. This is your chance to practice compassion, unconditional love, and vision-casting with the women you encounter in your daily life.

That's how the Christian life works: We draw apart to be with God, then we go back into the world to love as we have been loved.

If you're meeting with a group, one woman will need to take responsibility for facilitating the discussion at each meeting. You can rotate this responsibility or let the same person facilitate all six sessions. The facilitator's main task is to keep the discussion moving forward and to make sure everyone has a chance to speak. This will be easiest if you limit the size of your discussion group to no more than eight people. If your group is larger than eight (especially in a Sunday school class), consider dividing into subgroups of four to six people for your discussion.

Spiritual influence is not just for super-Christians. You can make a difference in someone's life by letting God work through you. Take a chance—the results may surprise you!

1

WHAT'S IMPORTANT?

We were both afraid to open the Tupperware in our refrigerators. We were both guilty of spraying deodorant on dirty sox and throwing them into the dryer on AIR FLUFF. We discovered that while one of us was trying to quick-dry Jockey shorts in the microwave oven (they disappear, all but the waistband) the other one was frantically thawing frozen steaks in the dishwasher (full cycle; no soap).

—PAM YOUNG AND PEGGY JONES [1]

I committed my life to Christ as a child, and I grew up wanting to please Him. For me that meant doing *more* for Him. So when an invitation came to be the chairperson for a local Christian women's luncheon, I said I'd be happy to do it. Along with that commitment came extra meetings and numerous weekly phone calls. When someone was needed to teach a Bible study, I quickly committed two days a week to the leaders' meeting and the teaching day. I also had Little League games for my son, business dinners with my husband, and responsibilities to everyone I knew.

I started resenting my family and friends because I could tell the more I did for them, the more they expected. And I was exhausted! An incident I wrote about in *Tame Your Fears* brought me face to face with how out of balance my life was:

I jumped out of bed early, showered, dressed hurriedly, and sat reading the paper at the kitchen table while enjoying a freshly brewed cup of coffee.

J. P. (Jason Paul) came downstairs a few minutes later. I made him some breakfast and returned to my coffee. Minutes later while peering at me over his cereal bowl, he said, "Mama, you look so pretty today."

I couldn't believe it. On most days I'm quite dressed up. . . . On the day in question, I had dressed for leisure— nothing special, just slacks and a sweater.

We made eye contact, and I questioned him: "Honey, why do you think I look pretty today? These are old clothes, and usually Mother's wearing something nicer."

He flashed his gorgeous blue eyes and smiled at me. "It's because," he said thoughtfully, "when you're all dressed up, I know you're going out some place, but when you look like this, I know you're all mine!"[2]

Soon after this incident I got on my knees and offered my precious day planner to God. This detailed calendar had everything in it that made me feel like I was accomplishing worthwhile tasks with my life. But as I analyzed my heart, I realized most of the commitments on that calendar were activities that made me look important, spiritual, or valuable to other people. I confessed to God that my motive in saying yes to too many things wasn't really for Him; it was to make me feel good in front of other people. In this first session we'll look at how Jesus answered the question, "What's important?" We'll see how central the idea of the *heart* is in His answer. We'll examine our own priorities in light of this teaching and begin to put our life purpose into words. You'll need paper and pens for this session.

1. Brainstorm a list of funny and not-so-funny ways you could complete this sentence:

   I know my life is out of balance when _____.

   ("I know my life is out of balance when my child gives me a Mother's Day card he made himself, and I didn't realize it was already May." "I know my life is out of balance when I can't find my Bible." "I know my life is out of balance when I find my lost Bible — under a pile of laundry washed last week but still not folded." "I know my life is out of balance when the voice on my e-mail system says, 'You've got mail!' and I start to cry.")

2. What is one *serious* question you have about maintaining a balanced life? (If you have several burning questions, go ahead and list them all.)

What's important? What's really important in life? Many business consultants urge individuals and corporations to have a purpose or mission statement, a clear expression of why they exist and where they're going. Matthew 22:34-40 tells what Jesus says should be in everyone's purpose statement.

3. Read Matthew 22:34-40. According to Jesus, what should be our top priority? How would you state it in your own words?

4. Priority number two is really two priorities in tension with each other: "Love your neighbor as yourself." How is this different from each of the following alternatives?

Love your neighbor as you love God.

Love your neighbor more than you love yourself.

Love yourself more than you love your neighbor.

We might depict this system of priorities in a set of concentric circles:

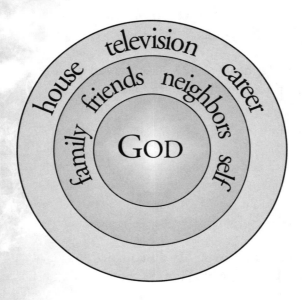

5. What do you think it means, in practice, to love God with everything in you—more than you love your family, your friends, your ministry, your career, or yourself? If that were your heart's priority, how might it play itself out in your choices and actions?

6. What is one situation in which you feel the tension between loving yourself well and loving another person or persons well?

In many ways our culture teaches us to value material possessions more than people. However, in Matthew 6:19-21,24, Jesus critiques the love of things.

7. Read Matthew 6:19-21,24. How can the love of possessions throw our lives out of balance?

How Can I Discover My Purpose?
In earlier days, I thought God's purpose was that I should say yes to every opportunity to help people. Now I know that I need a focused sense of my unique purpose so that I can say yes to the right things and no to the rest.

Six Steps to Clarify Your Calling in this series takes a deeper look at finding your life's purpose. For now, take five minutes on your own to think about these two questions:

8. What makes you weep and pound the table?

As you look at your growing-up years, your young-adult years, and your life today, what are you passionate about? What do you long to be involved in? What are your hopes and dreams for the future? What brings you a sense of indignation or an exhilarating ability to see the possibilities in a situation or a person? Is it working with children, introducing others to Christ, meeting the needs of the homeless, seeking justice for the downtrodden, righting a wrong in society, or organizing people? The list is limitless. Write down a few things that come to your mind.

9. What unique gifts do you have?

Be honest about compliments you've received. Has someone told you that you have outstanding administrative ability? Are you an excellent teacher or writer? Are you good at telling stories that make a point or asking questions that spark discussion? Do you have a flair for decorating? Do people respond to the gospel when you share your faith? Are you able to "read" where people are coming from? Are you a natural-born encourager? Do you find it a privilege to intercede in prayer for others? Do you have creative talents? Musical gifts? Athletic abilities? People skills? Are you often the leader in a group you are with? Write down any gifts you know God has blessed you with. If nothing comes to mind, write down some ways people have complimented you. (Remember, God often uses the compliments of people to affirm your gifts.)

10. If you're meeting with a group, share what you came up with for questions 8 and 9. What was it like for you to consider these two questions?

This is a first step toward putting your purpose into words. If you had trouble, don't despair! Many women start out with no idea of what is important to them. You may want to come back to these questions over a period of time, praying about your purpose and reading the Bible in search of God's purposes. When life begins to feel out of balance, you can ask yourself, "What's important?"

In *Six Steps to Clarify Your Calling*, you can follow a process of creating a purpose statement. Whenever I am asked to do another activity, I place the invitation alongside my purpose statement and decide if it fits. If the answer is no, I know someone else should do that job. If the answer is "I'm not sure," I take time to pray about it and ask God to reveal His will to me. Having a purpose statement has been the most freeing experience of my Christian life!

Here are some sample purpose statements:

- My purpose is to draw myself and others into an ever-deeper experience of God's community of joy. (Karen)
- The purpose of my life is to bring out the best in myself and other people by loving, learning, leading, and living joyfully. (Cindy, a friend of ours)
- My purpose is to illuminate and inspire hurting people everywhere with the knowledge and application of God's truth. (Joy, my sister)
- My purpose is to evangelize, equip, encourage, and empower people to impact others with their God-given potential. (mine)

A woman doesn't have to choose between having a purpose in life and being a faithful and fun-loving mom, wife, and friend. One of the best things we can contribute to the people we love is to be a woman who responds to the call of God. Through us, those we love experience the joy of following God and are often challenged to consider their own God-infused purposes.

—JAN JOHNSON[3]

11. What might be the next step for you in clarifying what is important in your life?

If you're meeting in a group, pair up with a partner. Share with each other your answers—or your struggles!—for questions 8 and 9. Write down some notes that will help you know how to pray for your partner.

Regather with the rest of the group. Pray for your partner to discover God's purposes for her life. If you'd like, you can simply pray, "Lord, *Name* wants to align the purpose her life with what you think is important. Please enable her to . . . "

Tape your notes about your partner's passions and gifts to the inside cover of this booklet. Each day this week, ask God to reveal to your partner her purpose and enable her to fulfill it. Ask God to enable you to fulfill your purpose.

Commit to reading one chapter of the gospel of Luke every day, asking yourself, "What are God's purposes? What does God want done?" Write a few sentences of notes each day about what you observe.

Part of the purpose of each Christian is to influence the people around her in positive ways. Even if your life feels crazy, you have at least one small thing to offer another person each week.

Snag a minute to phone or e-mail your prayer partner. Share with her what you're realizing about what's important in life. Rejoice with her over what she's learning. Encourage her that somewhere in all the craziness of her life, she has a purpose for existing!

> *I love to accomplish great and noble tasks, but it is my chief duty and joy to accomplish humble tasks as though they were great and noble.*
>
> —HELEN KELLER[4]

2

CAN I DO IT ALL?

I've learned that balance does not mean we are good at everything. It means we do what we do well and get help with the rest. It means we do not make the mistake of lighting the candle at both ends and putting a match to the middle. One of the definitions of balance is the power or ability to decide. Well, we all have that.

—LIZ CURTIS HIGGS[1]

I was finishing the residence hours for my master's degree. I had taken stimulating classes in acting, interpersonal relationships, set design, and public speaking. After teaching high school drama, speech, and English for four years, I already knew how to communicate effectively with students, but these new classes gave me ideas for updating my lesson plans and stimulating my students' thinking. I could hardly wait to get back into the classroom.

However, I had a major decision to make. I was seven-and-a-half months pregnant, and going back to teaching in the fall would mean all-day childcare for my newborn. I was earnestly looking forward to my baby's birth, but I also loved my students and had a strong commitment to my role as teacher and to the self-esteem it brought me. And of course, there were my paycheck and benefits to consider. After much prayer and heart-wrenching conversations with my husband and others, I made the difficult choice to take an indefinite leave of absence from teaching.

A few weeks after this decision, school started and I wasn't there. The paychecks had stopped, finances were tight, and I was second-guessing my decision. My feelings ran the gamut:

- *Denial*—I don't really feel bad about not going back to school. I don't miss it at all!
- *Anger*—If I just hadn't listened to my husband and friends say how important it would be for me to bond with my baby during those first few months. They don't understand how important my job is to me!
- *Bargaining*—If I stay home the first three months after the baby is born, maybe I can go back to teaching after the first of the year. That will make my husband and my mother feel better, and I still won't miss teaching for the whole year.
- *Depression*—I am so alone. I'm probably the only woman alive who feels so miserable. I think everybody would be better off if I just disappeared.

Sometimes saying no to something that looks desirable allows us to say yes to a greater purpose, even if we don't see it at the time. Once my baby was born, I was thrilled that I had decided to stay home. I could return to teaching later, but for now, my life was committed to something else.

Your balancing act no doubt involves different choices than mine, but many of us are staggering under the load of "shoulds" life piles on us: career, home, relationships, children's activities, ministry, exercise, and on and on. In this session, we'll ask, "Can I do it all?" and learn how Jesus answered this question through His purpose statements and His choices. You'll need 3x5 cards (at least ten per person) and pens for this session.

> *How we spend our days is, of course, how we spend our lives . . . There is no shortage of good days. It is good lives that are hard to come by.*
>
> —ANNIE DILLARD [2]

1. Give a stack of 3x5 cards to each woman in the group. Each person needs about ten cards and something with which to write. Take a few minutes on your own to write on each card *one major consumer of your time and energy.* For example, you might write "sleep" on one card and "interacting with children" on another. Try to come up with about six to ten different items.
2. Look at each card in your stack. For each one, take a minute and think about what your life would be like without this item. For instance, without sleep, you'd be mentally ill or dead. (Maybe you've already had a taste of this.) Picture yourself without each item.
3. Perhaps life doesn't look good minus any one of the items you've identified. But if you had to live without one of them, which would you choose to drop? Talk to the group

about why you chose the one you did and how it feels to make this choice.

> *Purpose is the framework of life that enables us not only to say we desire to be God's woman . . . but to become God's woman. It keeps us from being crushed with failure and egotistical with success; it gives us the know-how to steer our way through tough decisions.*
>
> —SHEILA WEST [3]

Saying no to something good is painful; maybe that's why we do it so seldom! But life forces us to make those choices often. Our purpose statement can help us. Jesus stated His own purpose in a number of ways.

4. Read the following passages. What elements did Jesus include in His purpose?

Luke 4:18-19

Luke 5:32

Luke 19:10

5. What are some legitimate life goals that are not a part of Jesus' purpose?

While He didn't get wrapped up in the precise wording of His purpose statement, Jesus was very clear on His life's focus. This clarity enabled Him to say no to things that might have been good but weren't essential to His purpose. He didn't aspire to being a leader in His local synagogue because His mission was to sinners, not to the righteous. Once He began His preaching ministry, He apparently paid little attention to earning a living or maintaining a household. He chose not to marry or have children. He invested His energy in relationships with a small group of disciples and offended His relatives by having correspondingly little time for them. By many modern standards, Jesus' life wasn't balanced; it was focused and limited. He didn't try to do it all.

Healing was a large part of Jesus' mission, but He didn't even try to heal everyone.

6. Read Luke 4:40-44. What priorities did Jesus focus on?

7. In what ways did Jesus place limits on His life in this passage?

Becoming human meant that Jesus had limits. He needed food and sleep. He couldn't preach His message in Jerusalem on Monday, Rome on Tuesday, and China on Wednesday. Maybe through a miracle He *could* have done this, but He didn't try. Except for the occasional hike across the Sea of Galilee, He accepted His human limits. In fact, He *welcomed* the limits He received from His Father. When the Devil tried to get him to defy the law of gravity in order to prove that His Father would rescue Him, Jesus refused (see Matthew 4:1,5-7).

8. Read John 5:19 and 5:30. What do you think Jesus meant when He said He could do only what He saw His Father doing?

9. How would your life be different if instead of saying, "I can do it all," you said, "I can do only what I see my Father doing"?

10. Many of us can hardly sleep at night knowing how much we've left undone. Do you think Jesus lay awake feeling guilty that so many people were still sick or hadn't heard the gospel? What makes you say that?

Jesus accepted limits regarding family, friends, career, and ministry. Far from dooming Him to a life of mediocrity, His acceptance of limits freed Him to please His Father and to do what He saw His Father doing.

Our unique purpose may put different limits on us than the ones Jesus had. For example, Jesus chose not to have a spouse or children. We may be called to marriage and children. Jesus lived for several years off the donations of people to whom He ministered. We may need to work for wages. Our different purposes may lead to *different* limits, but they don't mean *no* limits.

11. What goes through your mind when you think about living within limits?

> The difference between "peak performers" and "pace addicts," research confirms, is that the peak performer acquires this ability to stand back, reflect, and reconsider, whereas the pace addict is forever preoccupied with the frenzy of the moment . . . She becomes addicted to an artificial high that leaves her flat and despairing.
>
> —PAULA RINEHART[4]

Overcoming Drivenness

Once we discover we *can't* "do it all," we need to figure out how to redirect our thinking. Drivenness as a lifetime habit is challenging to overcome. Releasing our grip on the need "to do" in order to feel good about ourselves is essential. Here are some suggestions:

- *Realize your value comes from God,* not from your personal achievements. Take a five-minute break in the middle of each workday to breathe slowly and meditate on this truth.
- *Release the "frenzy of the moment."* If the job you are doing takes twice as long to get done, it will still get done—perhaps even more effectively.
- *Rebuild relationships* weakened by busyness. Mark time on your calendar for nurturing important friendships, and keep those dates as definitely as if they were your most important appointments—because they are!
- *Reestablish your spiritual balance* by setting aside a specific amount of time each day to read God's Word, pray, and ask for His direction.

> *God will not ask how many books you have read or how many miracles you have worked; He will ask you if you have done your best, for the love of Him.*
>
> —MOTHER TERESA[5]

Take your stack of 3x5 cards and spread them out before God. If you're meeting with a group, you'll have a great mess of cards among you, perhaps spread out on the floor. Offer to God all the things that keep you busy. Acknowledge God as the Creator who made you with limits. Ask Him to show each one of you what you need to do less and what you need to do more.

Write a letter to God telling Him exactly what you think about your limits. If you'd like, complain! *How am I supposed to fulfill my purpose when I need so much sleep, when I have only so much money, when I was born so shy (or so expansive)?! What were You thinking?!* Or, you can thank God for your limits. If the idea of limits feels . . . well, limiting, you can tell God you refuse to believe you're limited. Say whatever is on your mind.

Look again at your purpose statement, as well as your partner's. Ask God to show you how to live your purpose today.

Call someone in your group and ask her what she's thinking about this idea of limits. Ask her how you can pray for her.

> *The great doing of little things makes the great life.*
>
> —EUGENIA PRICE [6]

3

Is God
Trustworthy?

The statement that God is in control is either true or it's not true. If it's not true, we'd better forget about God. But if it is true and we accept God's revelation of Himself, our faith enables us to enjoy and rest in the certainty of His providence.

—Paul Little[1]

Behind much of our life's imbalance lurks a question: Is God trustworthy? Consider my case:

The day I miscarried my second child I was on my way to a speaking engagement. During the drive my abdominal cramps became so severe there was no question that something had gone awry. Arriving at my destination, a community center, I headed for the ladies' room. Graffiti covered the walls and disgusting smells permeated the vulgar stall. It was over in a moment. I knew I was no longer pregnant.

After an intense moment of emotion, I took care of my immediate physical needs and my mind clicked into gear. In the next room, over two hundred women were waiting for their speaker. I gathered all my strength and walked into the banquet room.

The relieved chairperson saw me entering the room and announced, "Our speaker has finally found our location! We're so thankful you made it. Ladies, let's welcome Carol Kent!" I stepped up to the stage. Directly in front of me, three rows back, was a mother holding her infant. My mind went blank and my empty arms were numb.

Thoughts swirled in my mind: *I am so angry with God! How cruel of Him to let me lose my baby! How could a God of love let me miscarry the baby I wanted so much and then put a woman with a newborn right in front of me when I'm supposed to be giving an inspiring talk about how great He is?*

Pulling myself together, I delivered my prepared speech and stumbled through good-byes at the end of the luncheon. With my characteristic "controlling" demeanor, I left that group without expressing my loss to anyone. But I sobbed all the way home—alone in my car—intermittently verbalizing my angry feelings toward God.

Two hours later as my car pulled into my driveway, I turned off my emotions. Apart from my husband, no other family members or friends knew about the pregnancy yet, so there was no need to tell them anything. I decided the easiest way to cope would be to pretend it never happened. I threw myself into my work—any worthy ministry or community activity had my attention. If I kept myself busy enough, I didn't have to think about my pain, and I was so tired at night, I could sleep. But I soon found out this method of coping with my hidden questions about God's trustworthiness didn't work!

Doubting God's goodness often throws our lives out of balance. In my case, mistrust led me to bury myself in projects, relationships, and causes. Another woman might work too much because she mistrusts God's ability to provide for her physical needs. Another might spend too much time shuttling children to activities because she doesn't trust God to raise them into successful adults unless they are musicians, athletes, or academic stars.

Can God be trusted to provide what we most deeply need, or do we have to wear ourselves out providing for ourselves? Is the universe essentially a safe place where we can relax or a scary place where we must be constantly on alert? In this session, we'll see how Jesus answered such questions not just for our heads, but also for our hearts. You'll need paper and pens for this session. You'll also need a piece of stovetop-safe cookware and a book of matches.

1. What is one reason you have for believing that God is good?

When we don't trust that God is willing and able to meet our deepest needs, then we can become angry, depressed, or anxious. Any of these three responses can fuel frenzied activity, but Jesus had the most to say about anxiety.

Most of His audience lived on the edge of destitution. They were manual laborers and shopkeepers. The Roman government was crushing them with impossible taxes. If anyone had reason to mistrust God and worry about survival, they had.

2. Read Matthew 6:25-34. Describe the out-of-balance life that Jesus portrays in this passage.

3. What does Jesus urge people to trust about God in this passage?

4. Think of the busiest person you know. What would he or she say in response to what Jesus says here about God?

5. Read Matthew 7:7-12. What reasons for trusting God does Jesus offer here?

It's easier to believe Jesus' words in our heads than in our hearts. Deep down where it counts, we can mistrust God's *goodness:* His willingness to provide the food, clothes, love, security, and meaning that we need. We can also mistrust God's *power:* His ability to provide for us, or His *wisdom:* His understanding of what we need.

6. How might a person's tendency to work too hard at a job be related to a lack of trust in God's goodness, power, or wisdom?

7. How might a person's tendency to work too hard at ministry be related to a lack of trust in God's goodness, power, or wisdom?

8. These days, some mothers worry about getting their children into the right preschool, grade school, soccer camp, or college. What do you think Jesus would say to these mothers?

9. Trust doesn't happen just because we know we *should* trust God. What are some reasons why a person might not trust God to provide what she most deeply needs? (For instance, what if she feels she's been asking for bread and getting only stones?)

10. Give each woman a sheet of paper and a pen. Take five minutes to make a list of everything you worry about. "If I don't _____, then _____?" "What if _____?" "I'm worried that _____." If you're worried that your worries are stupid or unspiritual, or that God won't love you if He knows you don't trust Him enough, write that down, too. If you genuinely don't think you're worried about anything, write a letter of thanks to God.

Relying on God has to begin all over again every day as nothing yet had been done.

—C. S. LEW

What Settles the Trust Issue?

When I'm struggling with trust issues, it can be as challenging as my miscarriage or as simple as the nagging worry about whether my child will make it home from school safely. If I'm honest, I'm really dealing with one of the following three issues:

- Will I trust God to meet my need (or my family's need), or will I obsess about controlling the uncontrollable?
- Will I choose a constant level of anxiety about the situation, or will I tell God about my challenge and leave it in His hands?
- Will I avoid dealing with the real issue by escaping into activities, relationships, ministry, novels, the Internet, shopping, unnecessary "white-glove" housecleaning, or any number of other options?

The most helpful advice about trust I ever encountered was the testimony of Corrie ten Boom. She, her father, and her sister, Betsie, were imprisoned during the Second World War for rescuing Jews. Corrie's father died. While in solitary confinement, Betsie wrote, "This horror has come to us from God's loving hands to purify me."[3] Later, Corrie wrote, "We are in God's training school and learning much. We are continually protected by the most extraordinary providence, and we know that we can hold out in spite of the hard life. God knows the way; we are at peace with everything."[4] For Betsie, the cell door was unlocked when God took her home. Corrie, released from the concentration camp shortly thereafter due to a clerical error, said, "I became a tramp for the Lord, going wherever I could tell what I had learned: that when the worst happens in the life of a child of God, the best remains, and the very best is yet to be."[5]

Corrie and Betsie had settled the question in their minds—
God is good and *He is trustworthy.* They had an eternal perspective,
and it freed them to stay totally balanced in the middle of uncertain circumstances.

> *As we grow in trusting God in all things, our contentment
> becomes an act of worship. . . . Peace wraps around your
> heart when you're able to trust God for just today and not
> be burdened with the If Onlys, the What ifs, and the
> Whys . . . Your questions are for His safekeeping . . . your
> freedom [produces] an ability to concentrate on others and
> their needs, to encourage others, to love and serve the
> people God brings into your life.*
>
> —LINDA DILLOW[6]

Put all of your written worries into a piece of cookware—something that can tolerate a flame. You can crumple them or tear
them up if you'd like. Set the cookware on a table or the floor in
the middle of your group (you may want to set it on a
potholder). Let one person introduce your time of prayer by saying something like "Father, we want to offer all of our worries to
You. . . . " Then let someone light a match and set your worries on
fire. While your worries burn, or after a moment of silence, offer
any other prayers you have. The leader can close in a final prayer.

Meditating on Scripture is a way of letting its truth sink deep
into your heart, changing the way you think and feel about

things. Meditating is like chewing on something long enough to derive the full flavor of it. One way to do this is to imagine yourself in one of the biblical stories. Matthew 8:23-27 describes Jesus and His disciples during a storm.

Find a place where you can be undisturbed for ten minutes. (If you have small children, that may be asking a lot!) Sit comfortably with your back straight and your feet flat on the floor. Take a couple of slow, deep breaths to clear your head. Read Matthew 8:23-27 aloud. Imagine yourself in the scene as you read it. Picture yourself as one of the disciples in the boat. Feel the boat tossing in the waves, taste the salt in the air, and hear your fellow disciples becoming agitated. If you sense the Holy Spirit say, "Stop and pay attention," reread a key sentence, or close your eyes and imagine yourself in the boat at that point. Let the scene play out as a movie in your mind, with you as a character in the movie.

If you don't sense anything from the Holy Spirit, read the story to yourself again. Let yourself feel what the disciples might have felt when the waves crashed into the boat, when they were waking Jesus, when He scolded them for lacking faith, and when He calmed the storm with a word. Imagine yourself in that calm boat. Let the scene sink into your heart. Or if the words of Jesus or the disciples strike you more than the pictures, repeat those words to yourself and ask, *What does God want me to hear in these words?*

Do you know someone who is currently questioning God's trustworthiness? It may be someone in your group or outside it. If so, phone her or send her a note. Tell her something you learned from your study this week. Don't lecture ("Here's what you need to know." "Here's what you should do."). Instead, tell her something you realized about yourself or about God.

If the worries you burned are still hanging around, don't keep them to yourself. Call someone in the group and say, "Here's my worry. Will you help me think of something constructive I can do with it?"

> *Worry does not empty tomorrow of its sorrow, it empties today of its strength. It does not enable us to escape evil. It makes us unfit to face evil when it comes. It is the interest you pay on trouble before it comes.*
>
> —CORRIE TEN BOOM [7]

4

ARE WE HAVING FUN YET?

Laughter is the corrective force which prevents us from becoming cranks.

—HENRI BERGSON [1]

TENSION filled the air. My husband had taken over some of the management of my ministry and had moved his office in with mine, but the adjustments of working side by side were substantial. It was fun to be together for spontaneous walks or bike rides along the river. However, I also had to relinquish some control. Often, there was friction as I resisted his attempts to change what I thought were perfectly effective procedures.

I was finishing up a manuscript against a looming deadline. I had not taken many breaks from my intense work, and my responses to Gene's questions were a little snippy. The next morning I took my coffee cup to my office, and on the top of the desk I noticed my day planner open to the following week. In the square that said April 21 (my birthday) there was a big hand-drawn red heart with an arrow through it. It read: "C. J. (Carol Joy) + G. K. (Gene Kent)." Under the heart, Gene had written: "Carol's birthday with Gene—

5 P.M. to midnight." I smiled, knowing my romantic husband had not forgotten my special day.

Tuesday arrived, and I eagerly dressed up for my 5:00 P.M. date, which I assumed would be a lovely dinner in a local restaurant. To my surprise, my administrative assistant, Laurie, and her husband, Tom, showed up in the driveway to go with us. Instead of going to my favorite eatery, Gene drove toward the expressway. We were headed for Detroit. Then he turned off the highway and onto an inner-city street. Within two blocks, I heard the other three passengers in the car squeal, "We're *here!*" But *where* were we? My special birthday dinner had been planned at McDonald's! The men wore suits, and Laurie and I were in party attire and high heels.

As we waited in line to order our burgers, we were quite a sight for the other fast-food patrons! We laid out our dinner at our special "table for four" and laughed out loud—and so did a lot of other people in the restaurant as they observed our unusual apparel. The joke had definitely been on me!

Upon leaving the restaurant, I soon learned what the *real* birthday surprise was—front-row theater tickets to *The Wizard of Oz,* starring Mickey Rooney! It was one of my favorite childhood stories. Our seats were so close to the stage we could practically touch the tail of the Cowardly Lion! Afterward we went out for more "sophisticated" food at an Italian restaurant and laughed some more. It was a *glorious* night—an unexpected interruption in my too-tense, rigid, never-take-a-break work mode.

The next morning I grabbed my coffee cup and sat down at the kitchen table next to my husband. "Honey, thank you for planning such a special birthday getaway for me," I said. "I almost forgot what it felt like to forget my deadlines and relax. It was wonderful!"

He placed his hand over mine and with twinkling eyes said, "You *need* me in your life! It *was* a great night and I think we're going to have a great day, too!" And it was. The positive turning point in our close working arrangement was that night of *fun*. I quit taking everything so seriously and began to relax, trusting Gene and Laurie with the office details, so I could be free to meet my deadlines without so much pressure.

The moral of the story is this: If you are under stress and your life is out of balance, get all dressed up and go to McDonald's. Enjoy looking like an idiot. Make people smile. Act like nothing is wrong with your attire. Smile back at the people staring at you. Enjoy life! Do something uncharacteristic of your usual personality. Unwind.

Get ready to enjoy this session! We're going to explore the role of rest, relaxation, celebration, and exercise in a balanced life.

1. What have you done that was fun or relaxing during the past couple of weeks?

In Jesus' day, people didn't have to go out of their way to get exercise. Most people, men and women, did a great deal of manual labor and walked everywhere they went. It's no surprise, then, that no Bible verse commands, "Thou shalt get off thy couch."

On the other hand, people did have to go out of their way to rest. Jewish law required people to work for six days and rest on the seventh; they were supposed to give their servants the day off as well. Good Jews regarded those who worked on the Sabbath as "sinners," but there were a lot of "sinners" who couldn't imagine making ends meet if they abandoned their farms, businesses, and household chores for a full day. Roman law had no rules about days off, so nonJews got holidays only for religious festivals— literally, "holy days."

The Bible records no instances in which Jesus laughed, but a lot of times when He told funny stories. Did Jesus laugh?

Jesus often took time away from work to pray (more on that in session 6). But did He rest? Relax? Take time to enjoy people and the created world? Tell a joke and let loose with a roar of laughter? Or did He have serious business on His mind all the time? First, let's consider the rumor that Jesus was a friend of tax collectors and sinners.

2. What picture of Jesus' lifestyle do you get from the following passages?

   Mark 2:14-20

   Luke 7:31-35

3. When Jesus went to dinner with Levi and his "sinner" friends, do you think He did it only for ministry, or do you imagine Him enjoying the party? What makes you say that?

4. What role does eating and drinking with friends and other sinners play in your life? Why do you suppose that's the case?

What about the Jewish rhythm of work and rest? As good Jews, Jesus and His disciples lived by the Ten Commandments, including the command,

> Remember the Sabbath day by keeping it holy. Six days you shall labor and do all your work, but the seventh day is a Sabbath to the LORD your God. On it you shall not do any work, neither you, nor your son or daughter, nor your manservant or maidservant. . . . (Exodus 20:8-10)

However, Jesus did dispute interpretations of the Sabbath law that had developed over the centuries. The Pharisees and other strict interpreters had devised precise lists of activities that counted as "work" and so were forbidden on the Sabbath.

5. Read Mark 2:23–3:6. The Pharisees held that even picking a bit of grain for lunch was forbidden on the Sabbath because it was technically work. How did Jesus justify allowing His disciples to do this on the Sabbath?

6. The Pharisees also viewed healing as work. How did Jesus justify His decision to heal on the Sabbath?

7. Notice that Jesus did not say in either of these cases, "The Sabbath is an outmoded custom." He said, "The Sabbath was made for man" (2:27). How would you express Jesus' approach to the Sabbath in your own words?

8. Why do you think God commanded His people to take one day out of seven to rest?

9. In the Ten Commandments, God places Sabbath rest on the same level as avoiding adultery and murder. What do you make of that? Why make such a big deal over rest?

10. When we say we don't have time to spend each week worshiping God, enjoying our families and friends, and relaxing, what does that say about . . .

our trust in God to provide for us?

our love for our "neighbors"?

our belief about what is most loving for ourselves?

11. Read Matthew 11:28-30. In order to find true rest for our out-of-balance hearts and souls, Jesus says, "Come to me. . . . Take my yoke upon you . . . learn from me." What do you think these words mean in practical terms?

Many of us are addicted to activity. We fill every moment. Oh, we love to collapse in a chair with a magazine or watch mindless television to unwind. But the routine pace of our life is frantic. Have we become so accustomed to the busy status quo that we don't stop and reflect about how we really want to live? Are we trapped in jobs that drain the life out of us? Do we say yes to too many things?

—LOIS MOWDAY RABEY[2]

The Benefits of Fun, Relaxation, Rest, and Exercise

The Screwtape Letters is a satire in which the main character, a senior devil named Screwtape, gives instructions to his junior devil on how to defeat Christians. In one chapter, Screwtape warns about the dangers of fun:

> Fun is closely related to Joy—a sort of emotional froth arising from the play instinct. It is of very little use to us. It can sometimes be used, of course, to divert humans from something else which the Enemy [God] would like them to be feeling or doing: but in itself it has wholly undesirable tendencies; it promotes charity, courage, contentment, and many other evils. [3]

The *real* Enemy would love to keep us from enjoying our faith and from living happy, fulfilling Christian lives. I've found five reasons why fun, relaxation, rest, and exercise are beneficial:

- *We are healthier.* Dr. Nell Mohney says, "Laughter [and exercise] helps us to stay physically healthy and to fight disease. Laughter is like internal aerobics. Our circulation and heart rate are improved; our blood pressure is lowered; our immune system is strengthened; we are distracted from pain." [4]
- *We are more loving.* Being in a hurry always diminishes our capacity to love the people around us well. John Ortberg says, "Love always takes time, and time is the one thing hurried people don't have." [5]
- *We are kinder to our family and friends.* When I'm time-challenged, I speak sharp words to the people I love the most. My patience is thin, and I resent interruptions.

When I'm relaxed, I welcome interruptions as opportunities, and I speak kindly to my coworkers and family members.

- *We get more done.* If I've taken time for exercise, my mind is refreshed and I'm more creative. After breathing fresh air, I'm rejuvenated in mind and body. I accomplish more when I get back to my desk than I ever would have gotten done by mindlessly waiting for inspiration.
- *We are fun to live with.* When we are having fun, we don't take ourselves or those around us too seriously. William Kirk Kilpatrick once said, "Enter self-seriousness, exit humor. Exit humor, exit sanity."[6] The extra benefit is that nonChristians observe that our lives are enjoyable, happy, and balanced. This remarkable achievement opens the door for sharing our faith.

> *Jesus was often busy, but He was never hurried. Being busy is an outer condition; being hurried is a sickness of the soul.*
>
> —JOHN ORTBERG[7]

12. By the time you complete six sessions of a challenging Bible study, you may want to have a seventh gathering just for fun! Start planning it now. (You could even do something fun before your sixth meeting.) You could plan a party with your favorite foods, go to a show together, or do something active. A walk through botanical gardens? Horseback riding? Talk about what each group member finds relaxing and enjoyable.

·TALKING WITH GOD·

Allow a few minutes of silent prayer. At the beginning of your silence, have someone read Matthew 11:28-30 aloud. Let the words echo through your minds as you sit calmly together: "Come to me. . . . " Let the tension ooze out of your body, and breathe in Jesus' words slowly. After a few minutes of silence, the leader can either close with a brief prayer of her own, or you can let anyone who wants to pray aloud do so. If you choose to move into praying aloud, the leader should begin so that group members don't have to spend the silent time wondering who will break the silence.

·TIME ALONE WITH GOD·

Schedule an hour to do nothing—by yourself. Nothing means nothing: no books, no television, no food, no crafts, no "working out" athletically, no driving around—nothing. Don't pray in a concentrated way; just *be* with yourself and with God. If you can't think of any other way to get away from your kids for an hour, swap an hour of baby-sitting with someone else in your group. She needs an hour of nothing this week, too. Find someplace where you can be alone with little or no stimulation. Walk or sit or lie down under a tree. Be.

To get the full spiritual effect of doing nothing, you'll need at least half a day. Many of us need at least the first two hours to wind down and stop fidgeting. But if that seems impossible, an hour is a start. Afterward (not during your nothing time), think about what it would take to plan a half-day of nothing within the next six months.

You laugh: *How can doing nothing be spiritually nourishing?* Try it.

Tell someone what it was like to do nothing with God. Give her the truth. ("I never wanted to go home!" "My mind raced the whole time. I don't know how to do nothing.") Tell her you're trying to figure out how to get half a day with God in the next six months. Tell her any obstacles you face in fulfilling that plan, and ask for her encouragement. Chances are that just knowing you're seriously aiming for this goal will inspire her to consider penciling God into her day planner.

> *Seek to cultivate a buoyant, joyous sense of the crowded kindnesses of God in your daily life.*
>
> —ALEXANDER MACLAREN[8]

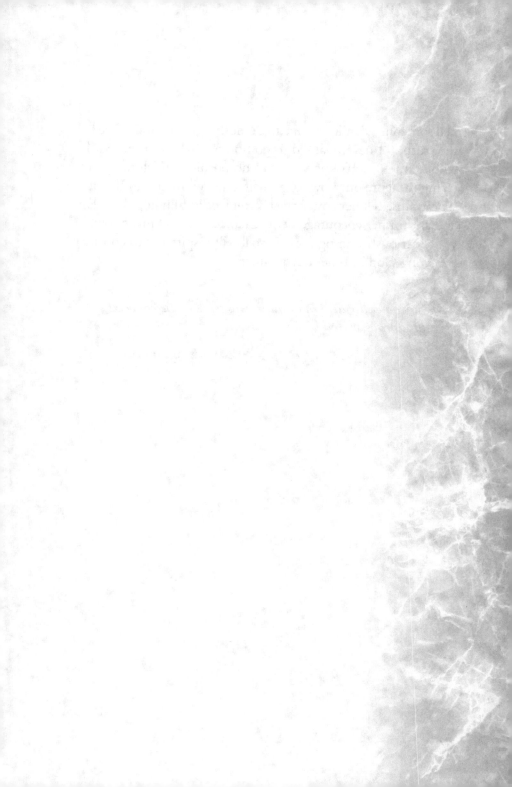

5

AM I ON MY OWN?

*You see we really do need each other, not because of
the inadequacies of God, but because this is the way
His grace works . . . God has made us this way.*

—REUBEN WELCH [1]

I was hosting my family for the holidays. That meant massive
housecleaning, rearranging closet space, getting beds ready for six-
teen overnighters, finding enough towels that still had matching
face cloths, buying and preparing food, and making sure every last
present was wrapped, tagged, and under the tree. Even with a helpful husband, it was exhausting. Between phone calls, a UPS
delivery, and a neighbor's visit, I was behind. The first carload would
be arriving in less than an hour. I turned around and couldn't believe
what I saw. My cat had puked on the white carpet. I was fuming
as I cleaned up the disgusting mess: *Why don't cats just digest their
hairballs? Why do we have a cat anyway? They have low IQs and always
act aloof. I feed this cat, provide a special low-fat diet, clean his litter
box, and I get thanked with this repulsive contribution to my holiday!*

My sisters had asked how they could help with preparations.
I let them bring some of the food, but instead of itemizing specific

ways they could take on major assignments, I told them I would take care of everything. Even a few days before our gathering, I brushed off their suggestions. I insisted, "Everything is under control."

Everything *wasn't* under control. I felt overworked, fatigued, and cranky! I won't even describe my spiritual condition. But when the first visitors arrived, I slapped on my happy face and greeted them warmly. Christmas carols were blaring from the CD player. Somehow they helped mask my *real* feelings.

After the rest of the family arrived, we sat down to eat at my perfectly set dining room table. The candles were lit and the food was enthusiastically consumed by hungry, happy people who were very excited about seeing each other.

Later, after cleaning up, I withdrew to a corner of the house that was still unoccupied. I was angry with myself. I was mad at my family for not *making* me accept their help. I was still upset with my cat for staining the carpet. And I wished the holidays didn't come as often as once a year! I wasn't blaming God because I was still rational enough to realize I had "done it to myself" by rejecting assistance. I had to confess my negative, controlling, I'll-do-it-myself attitude as sin and ask God's forgiveness.

Once that issue was settled, I decided to quit cleaning up after everybody and to let my sisters help with the dishes. I started *enjoying* my family. I walked into the family room and heard the sound of cousins laughing as they shook presents under the tree, trying to guess their contents. At a game table in the corner sat my mother and two sisters working on a jigsaw puzzle. The brothers-in-law were watching a movie and eating *again*. My dad was asleep in a chair. The Christmas lights twinkled, and in the background I thought I heard carolers singing, "Silent night, holy night, all is calm, all is bright . . ."

I've had to learn to let the people around me bring balance to my life. I love my independence, and sometimes I insist on it. But it's not what Jesus taught or modeled. In this session you'll explore how cultivating interdependence with other people can help you break habits of overwork and perfectionism that may unbalance your life.

1. What are some projects you've worked on in the past week (at home, at the office, in ministry) *alone?* If the answer is "none," you can say so.

2. What are some projects you've worked on in the past week *with others?* (Again, say "none" if appropriate.)

3. Do you tend most often to work on tasks alone or with others? Why do you think that's the case?

It is often difficult to ask for help. We may feel that no one else can accomplish the task the way we could, we may not want to inconvenience others, or we may feel too unworthy to be served. All these reasons are based on pride, and pride has no place in Christ's body.

—SUZANNE MANTHEI[2]

If ever there were someone who didn't need anyone's help, it would have been Jesus. Nobody could teach as well as Jesus; nobody could cast out demons or heal as well. Oddly, though, He took the earliest opportunity to select apprentices whom He trained and to whom He delegated increasing amounts of His job. These twelve apprentices are often known as the Twelve or the apostles ("sent ones").

4. Read Mark 6:6-13. What jobs did Jesus delegate to the Twelve in this passage?

5. Read Mark 6:30-44. When the Twelve returned from their travels, they "gathered around Jesus and reported to him all they had done and taught" (verse 30). Why do you think they did this?

6. Jesus took His apprentices away for a rest, but more work turned up. What tasks did He delegate to them this time?

7. Jesus could probably have performed all of these tasks as well as or better than the apostles. In fact, in the short run it was probably more work to train them than to do everything Himself. What might have been His reasons for giving the apostles some of the work? (What do you think His short-term goals were? What about His long-term goals?)

8. What do you think would have happened if Jesus had tried to do everything Himself? What would have happened to Jesus? To the ministry?

9. Many people have difficulty sharing or delegating work, especially when they are more qualified than others. Why do you suppose this is hard for some people to do?

10. How does this difficulty contribute to an unbalanced life?

We Can't Make It on Our Own
As women, we dislike being a "burden" to anybody. We're usually busy meeting somebody else's needs. But God designed us to need each other—and that brings balance to our lives physically, emotionally, and spiritually.

The key to solving this problem is to learn to interconnect:

- *Learn how to interconnect with God.* If we learn this principle first, interconnecting with people comes much more easily. Bob Benson writes,

     When I think of how little I bring, and how much He brings and that He invites me *to share [in His being]* . . . I am so filled with awe and wonder that I can hardly be heard. I know [I] don't have enough love or faith, or grace, or mercy or wisdom . . . but He has—He has all those things in abundance and says, *"Let's just put it all together. . . . Everything that I possess is available to you. Everything that I am and can be to a person, I will be to you."* [3]

- *Verbalize your need for help.* This is tough. It means putting your pride on the line. Ralph Keyes said, "Each one of us must take the hard, terrifying first step—saying to even one person—*I need you."* [4]
- *Don't dismiss others' generosity.* A controlling attitude robs others of the chance to grow by trying to do the task and to gain joy by offering you love.
- *Learn to delegate.* Jesus was a master at identifying the potential in His friends (the disciples), and He often gave them responsibilities and opportunities for ministry that might have felt way over their heads. But He allowed them the privilege of failing (if that's what it took) to learn a principle well. God may ask us to release our control of something we've been involved in for a long time so someone He has designed for future leadership can interconnect with us and grow spiritually as she tries something new.

The real barriers that hinder our relational intimacy come from within . . . fear and pride. Being vulnerable to another person is to most [people] a frightening experience. To expose their inner life would reveal that they do not have it all together. Many think they would be the only ones who did not.

—PAUL D. STANLEY AND J. ROBERT CLINTON [5]

11. Is there any area of your life in which delegating or asking for help would make things better in the long run? If so, what is that area?

12. What obstacles do you face in sharing your load with others?

Close with prayer. If you have difficulty asking for help, ask God to help you with this. If you have areas in your life in which you can't do everything, ask God to provide people to carry some of the load. Perhaps the leader would like to ask someone else to close in prayer!

Reflect on the tasks that consume your energy. What goes through your mind when you think about training someone else (even one of your children) to do part of it? What do you feel when you think about asking for help at church or at work? Offer your task list, along with these thoughts and feelings, to God.

What has it meant to you to have older Christian women come alongside and assist you with a project or help you define your dream? No matter what your age, pause for a moment and prayerfully consider who God wants you to connect with this week. (It might be your baby-sitter, someone you know from church, or someone you met at Bible study.) Write her name down. List her attributes. Make an appointment to get together with her this week and tell her the potential you've observed in her. Ask her if there is any way you can be of assistance as she pursues her current goals. Let her know you believe in her and want to be a cheerleader and a prayer supporter in her life.

6

Do I Enjoy God?

*Ahead of us lies the awesome privilege of delighting
in God if we will dare to draw near. . . . The result
for us will be similar to the experience of the biblical
saints: God's confidence, blessings, empowerment,
and joy during our lifetime.*

—Jerry Foote [1]

My quiet times were a disaster! I knew that in order to grow in my faith I needed to *do* devotions. I made myself get out of bed at 5:30 A.M. I was blurry-eyed and mentally challenged, but I opened my Bible to where I had left off the day before. I was going to read through the Bible in a year if it killed me—and it nearly did!

After my mandatory Scripture reading, I disciplined myself to pray for another thirty minutes, reading through an ever-growing list of requests that needed God's intervention. However, I had a problem. My mind wandered so much during my Bible reading that I often read the same page twice because it didn't sound familiar. I would never have been able to tell you what it said. Then I started falling asleep during my prayer time. My act of "doing devotions" was not even remotely devotional.

I decided to change my ways. My new method of spending time alone with God was to wait until I *felt* like it. I convinced myself that this was a far superior way to have intimacy with God because it would be a voluntary response of my heart, rather than a legalistic discipline. But to my surprise, I seemed to have less time than I did before. I was surprised that God didn't clear my schedule at a set hour every day so that we could be alone together. It never happened.

Then I met Helen. When she prayed aloud in small groups, she was talking to her best friend. When she read the Bible, it was as if she were reading a letter from someone who loved her. She taught me how to talk to God with my eyes wide open as I walked along the sidewalk. She reminded me to start my prayers with praise—to focus on everything God *is* and everything He has done—before I began my "gimme list" of what He could do for me. She also showed me how to journal my responses back to God through handwritten prayers after I read His Word. As I observed Helen and swallowed my pride enough to ask questions, I learned the difference between doing devotions out of obligation and being alone with God for the pure enjoyment of spending time together.

If you've ever struggled with the balance of time demands and the necessity of spending time with God, this session is for you. We'll look at the time Jesus spent alone with God and consider whether we view time with God as a duty or a pleasure.

1. When you're stressed or exhausted, what do you do to recharge your batteries?

2. Read the following passages. Make notes on anything you learn about Jesus' private life with the Father: *when* Jesus prayed, *where* He prayed, *how often* He prayed, and so on. Notice also what He was doing *before and after* He prayed.

Mark 1:35

Mark 6:45-46

Luke 5:15-16

Luke 6:12-13

3. What do you think motivated Jesus to spend a whole night praying?

4. Why do you suppose Jesus favored lonely, solitary places for prayer?

5. Do you think Jesus had to force Himself to make time for prayer? What makes you say that?

6. Imagine yourself spending all night praying. What would you have to believe (about yourself, God, prayer) in order to do that?

7. Describe your ideal prayer life. How much time would you like to spend with God in a typical month? What would happen during that time with God?

8. Many of us perceive a gap between the amount of time we'd like to spend in prayer and the amount we actually do spend. Many of us also perceive a gap between the intimate, intense experience of God we'd like to have in prayer and the actual experience we have when we pray. If you perceive a gap between your ideal and your actual prayer

life, what do you make of that? (For instance, do you feel like you've never learned *how* to pray? Do you think your priorities are flawed? Are your expectations unrealistic?)

9. Do you enjoy being alone with God? Honestly. If you do, talk about what you enjoy. If you don't, what do you think is missing?

Making Time Alone with God Enjoyable

Henri Nouwen talks about having a spiritual attitude that wants to be *surprised by God.* He says, "We crowd our thoughts with so many agenda items that we don't take time to listen to God. God doesn't just talk to me at the end or at the beginning of a project, but all the time; He may have me change directions in the middle."[2]

Here are five principles that will help you to experience the greatest pleasure you've ever known *alone* with Him.

- *Establish a time and place to spend time with God every day.* Write your appointment with God on your calendar as one of your official commitments of the day. My favorite place to meet with God is first thing in the morning in a faded rose-colored wingback chair in my office. When I sink into the feather cushion, I'm in a relaxed position for a meeting with my best friend. I often have a cup of coffee in my hand. In the beginning, your "appointment with God" may feel like an obligation you don't have time for, but that's okay. You may want to start by making this a fifteen-minute appointment, then gradually make it thirty minutes or longer. Establish some rules, such as *I will not answer the phone during this appointment. When my mind wanders and I think of all the laundry I have to do, I will not leave this appointment to put a batch of clothes in the washer.* If you *do* get interrupted by a screaming child or an emergency situation, when the crisis is over, go back to your original appointment with God.

- *Begin with a clean heart.* When I was a little girl, I didn't want to face my parents if I knew I had done something wrong and hadn't confessed it to them and asked for their forgiveness. I would hide, or surround myself with activities and other people, or avoid looking them in the eyes. It's the same with God. If we know we've disappointed Him by our attitudes or our actions, we avoid up-close and personal time with Him. So the first step to *enjoying* time with Him is to ask yourself: *Is there anything in my life right now that would be an embarrassment to my heavenly Father?* If the answer is yes, begin by confessing your sin to Him. This simple act of obedience will enable you to "look Him in the eyes" with joy instead of shame.

- *Express your love and appreciation for Him—out loud!* My personal time alone with God became a pleasure when I learned how to praise Him. I began by listing every name, attribute, and description of God I could think of. With my eyes open to my list while I talked to Him, my prayer went something like this:

Lord, You are the Creator—thank You for the beauty of the mountains and the oceans and the Great Lakes. You are my Savior, my Comforter, my Rock, my Shield, and my Great Reward. You are my Master; You're the God to Whom *nothing* is impossible. I love You more than these expressions of Your greatness can convey. Thank You for the gift of Your Son. Thank You for being my shelter in the middle of a stormy confrontation with my boss/husband/friend this week. What can I do today that would make You smile? I want to bring You the joy that You have already brought to me. I enjoy the pleasure of Your company.

The key to this principle is not to intersperse this part of your expression of praise, thanks, and adoration to Him with your list of what you want from Him.

- *Ask God to reveal a new truth to you about Himself each week—or to deepen a truth you've already known.* Carole Mayhall says,

I'll never forget one week in which I kept hearing God's voice saying one word to my soul. The word was *beloved.* All week He whispered that word to my heart, and it deepened my certainty of His love for me. When I was feeling useless, He would say, *Beloved.* When I was feeling harried, I'd hear Him whisper, *Beloved.* When I was anxious and cross, He would say it, too. All week long my heart heard Him until I felt loved. [3]

- *Talk to your best friend (God) about the needs you see in your world.* I started *enjoying* my time alone with God when I began *practicing His presence.* Sometimes I *listened* to Him as I meditated on what I read in His Word earlier in the day. I might be in my car, or in my home, or on a walk—usually with eyes wide open. Then as I moved through the day, I interceded in prayer for all of the people God put in my mind.

10. How important do you think it is that we enjoy God? When Jesus tells us to love God with all our heart, soul, and mind, do you think that love includes enjoyment, or is obedient service enough? What makes you say that?

11. What would it take for you to enjoy God more than you do now?

Convert your thoughts into prayer. As we are involved in unceasing thinking, so we are called to unceasing prayer. The difference is not that prayer is thinking about other things, but that prayer is thinking in dialogue. It is a move from self-centered monologue to a conversation with God.

—HENRI NOUWEN[4]

Take a moment to write down three reasons you have to praise God today.

When everyone is finished writing, close your eyes and imagine your heavenly Father looking at you with eyes of love and saying, "You are my beloved." What would you say in response to Him? Write it in the space below.

Use what you've written as the springboard for your group prayer. Say aloud as much or as little of it as you'd like. Instead of focusing on requests, focus on enjoying God's presence together.

Close by thanking God for the other women in your group. Thank Him for something specific about the woman on your right.

If yours is a life of rushing from one thing to the next, rushing into God's presence for fifteen minutes and rushing out again may not give you the experience of enjoying God. Take another look at your purpose statement. You've lived with it for a few weeks; feel free to make changes so that it expresses your life's purpose as well as it can. What do you *really* want? Where does God fit into that picture? Look at your calendar and find one thing that is less important to you than enjoying God. Say no to that item in order to say yes to one relaxed hour with your heavenly

Father. If home is too noisy, ask someone else to watch your kids for one hour while you escape with the One who loves you best. Find someplace solitary, even if it's just your car! Take a minute to rest in God's presence. Then start praising God for who He is and what He has done for you. If you need to cry or shed some anger or ask forgiveness first, that's okay.

Ask a friend if she enjoys being with God. Give her a chance to share honestly what is happening in her relationship with God. Listen without a superior attitude. Learn from what she says. Share your own experience with her, but *only* if she asks!

If you've been meeting with a group, buy an inexpensive box of cards and send a short note to each woman in your group. Thank her for opening her heart to you in the group. If you're good with words, say a lot. If you feel tongue-tied, it's enough to say, "You're terrific!"

> *It is in our time alone with Him that God not only orders our comings and our goings, but He also prepares us for them so that we can discern not only what we are to do, but what we are not to do. When we are with Him in the Word and in prayer, we gain understanding and wisdom that will sustain us and guide us in all other relationships.*
>
> —KAY ARTHUR[5]

NOTES

Chapter 1: *What's Important?*
1. Pam Young and Peggy Jones, *Sidetracked Home Executives* (New York: Warner Books, 1981), p. 10.
2. Carol Kent, *Tame Your Fears* (Colorado Springs, CO: NavPress, 1993), p. 185.
3. Jan Johnson, *Living a Purpose-Full Life* (Colorado Springs, CO: WaterBrook Press, 1999), p. 186.
4. Helen Keller, quoted by Billy and Janice Hughey, *A Rainbow of Hope* (El Reno, OK: Rainbow Studies, 1994), p. 53.

Chapter 2: *Can I Do It All?*
1. Liz Curtis Higgs, *Only Angels Can Wing It* (Nashville, TN: Nelson, 1995), p. 6.
2. Annie Dillard, quoted by Judy Couchman, *Designing a Woman's Life* (Sisters, OR: Multnomah, 1995), p. 15.
3. Sheila West, *Beyond Chaos* (Colorado Springs, CO: NavPress, 1991), p. 32.
4. Paula Rinehart, *Perfect Every Time* (Colorado Springs, CO: NavPress, 1992), pp. 167-168.
5. Mother Teresa, quoted by Cheri Fuller, *Quiet Whispers from God's Heart for Women* (Nashville, TN: J. Countryman, 1999), p. 88.
6. Eugenia Price, quoted by Terri Gibbs, editor, *Heartstrings* (Dallas, TX: Word, 1997), p. 38.

Chapter 3: *Is God Trustworthy?*
1. Paul Little, *How to Give Away Your Faith,* quoted by George Sweeting, *Great Quotes & Illustrations* (Waco, TX: Word, 1985), p. 252.
2. C. S. Lewis, quoted by Albert M. Wells, *Inspiring Quotations* (Nashville, TN: Nelson, 1988), p. 209.
3. Corrie ten Boom, *Clippings from My Notebook* (Minneapolis, MN: World Wide Publications, 1982), p. 18.
4. ten Boom, p. 18.
5. ten Boom, p. 19.
6. Linda Dillow, *Calm My Anxious Heart* (Colorado Springs: CO: NavPress, 1999), p. 192.
7. ten Boom, p. 33.

Chapter 4: *Are We Having Fun Yet?*
1. Henri Bergson, quoted by Becky Freeman, *Real Magnolias* (Nashville, TN: Nelson, 1999), p. 215.
2. Lois Mowday Rabey, *Snippets of Stillness,* quoted by Judith Couchman, *One Holy Passion* (Colorado Springs, CO: WaterBrook Press, 1998), p. 43.
3. C. S. Lewis, quoted by Earl Palmer, "Joy: Spiritual Health Made Visible," *Leadership,* Fall 1998, p. 36.

4. Dr. Nell Mohney, *How to Be Up on Down Days* (Nashville, TN: Dimensions for Living, 1997), p. 15.
5. John Ortberg, "Diagnosing Hurry Sickness," *Leadership,* Fall 1998, p. 31.
6. William Kirk Kilpatrick, quoted by Becky Freeman, p. 215.
7. John Ortberg, "Taking Care of Busyness," *Leadership,* Fall 1998, p. 30.
8. Alexander MacLaren, quoted by George Sweeting, *Great Quotes and Illustrations* (Waco, TX: Word, 1985), p. 123.

Chapter 5: *Am I on My Own?*
1. Reuben Welch, *We Really Do Need Each Other* (Nashville, TN: Impact Books, no date), pp. 37, 39.
2. Suzanne Manthei, "Learning to Receive," *Today's Christian Woman,* November/December 1991, p. 62.
3. Bob Benson, *Come Share the Being* (Nashville, TN: Impact Books, 1974), p. 106, italics mine.
4. Ralph Keyes, quoted by Benson, p. 73.
5. Paul D. Stanley and J. Robert Clinton, *Connecting* (Colorado Springs, CO: NavPress, 1992), pp. 176-177.

Chapter 6: *Do I Enjoy God?*
1. Jerry Foote, "Nearer than We Know," *Moody,* January/February 1997, p. 16.
2. Henri Nouwen, quoted in "Deepening Our Conversation with God," *Leadership,* Winter 1997, p. 115.
3. Carole Mayhall, *Come Walk With Me* (Colorado Springs, CO: WaterBrook Press, 1997), p. 15.
4. Henri Nouwen, quoted in "Deepening Our Conversation with God," *Leadership,* Winter 1997, p. 118.
5. Kay Arthur, *A Quiet Time Alone with God,* quoted by Judith Couchman, *One Holy Passion* (Colorado Springs, CO: WaterBrook Press, 1998), p. 46.

For information on scheduling Carol Kent or Karen Lee-Thorp as a speaker for your group, please contact Speak Up Speaker Services. You may call us toll free at (888) 870-7719, e-mail Speakupinc@aol.com, or visit our website at www.speakupspeakerservices.com.